Scratch IT

Teaching Primary Programming in Year 3

A research informed scheme of work by Phil Bagge HIAS Computing Inspector/Advisor
Part of the HIAS Teaching Primary Programming from Scratch Series

CONTENTS

A good plan might involve doing two or three of these modules in Year 3.
A Game followed by a nongame with Ladybug Munch to finish if pupils reading is good.

*These are simple games

INTRODUCTION & PROGRESSION

What Does This Book Do?

This book is a complete scheme of work for teaching primary programming using Scratch in Year 3 for 7–8 year olds.

What Is Included?

It includes permission to photocopy the pupil's worksheets answersheets and other resources that include this block for your class or school.

It includes links to example code, project templates and slides to improve how you introduce new programming concepts.

Part of a Series

It is part of a five book series. Three other books include projects for other year groups.

> *Scratch IT – Teaching Primary Programming in Year 4*
>
> *Scratch IT – Teaching Primary Programming in Year 5*
>
> *Scratch IT – Teaching Primary Programming in Year 6*
>
> *Teaching primary programming from 'Scratch' – Research informed approaches*

The teachers book listed at the end explores methodology and pedagogue in detail helping you to understand why an approach is useful.

Progression

There is a clear research informed progression through the series, and the graphic on the next page on a grey background shows which programming concepts are introduced in this book.

Pedagogue in a Few Paragraphs

Introduction to Programming Concepts Away From Code

Pupils are taught key programming concepts away from programming to lower cognitive load and make it easier to transfer these ideas from one programming language to another.

I Do You Do

While pupils are finding their way around the Scratch environment, we employ this basic methodology as it allows more solo hands on access.

PRIMM

Pupils are encouraged to read and understand code before they create their own code. We use the PRIMM method in this book in the last module.

Predict

Run

Investigate

Modify (change)

Make

Parsons

Some modules include a Parsons exercise to build code from teacher-provided pre-selected code.

Creative

Each project provides time and stimulus to be creative in code within the zone of proximal development provided by the taught concepts and explored projects. In other words, it has reasonable projects that can be created independently or with minimum teacher support.

Knowledge

Key knowledge is introduced in the concept introductions and reinforced in each of the activities.

Hints & Tips

The last module also includes a copy of the pupil resource annotated with extra information to further teachers programming knowledge, hints and formative assessment opportunities in case pupils are stuck and tips to adapt or support whole class teaching.

Many of this extra Hints and Tips will not be needed but the more informed the teacher is, the better quality learning opportunity pupils will have.

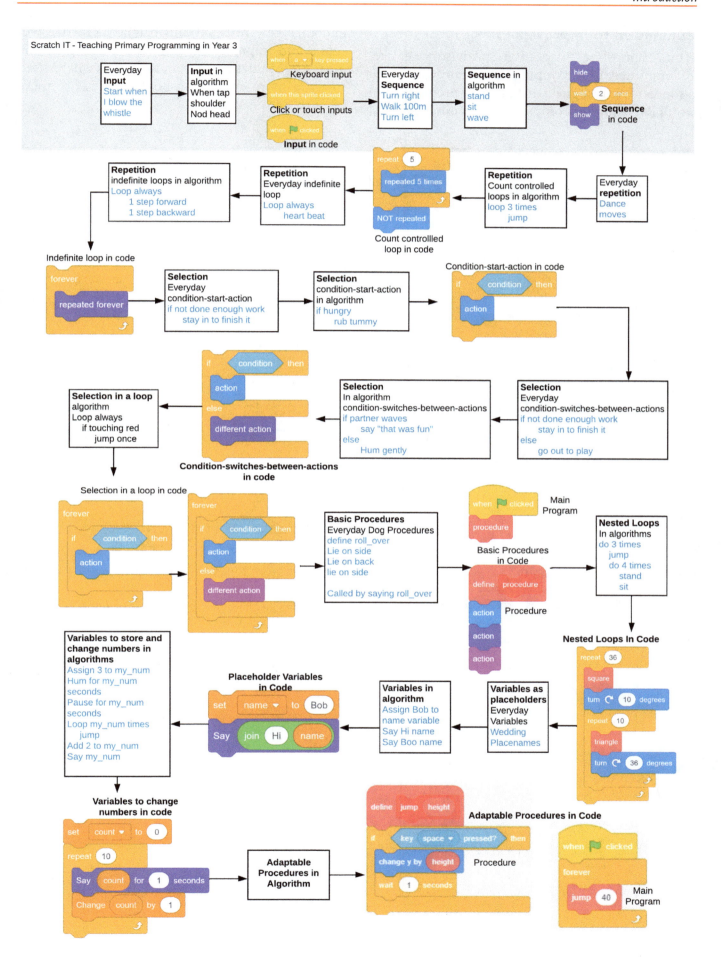

Scratch IT - Teaching Primary Programming in Year 3

Everyday Input
Start when
I blow the whistle

Input in algorithm
When tap shoulder
Nod head

Keyboard input

Click or touch inputs

Input in code

Everyday Sequence
Turn right
Walk 100m
Turn left

Sequence in algorithm
stand
sit
wave

Sequence in code

Everyday repetition
Dance moves

Repetition
Count controlled loops in algorithm
loop 3 times
    jump

Count controlled loop in code

Repetition
Everyday indefinite loop
Loop always
    heart beat

Repetition
indefinite loops in algorithm
Loop always
    1 step forward
    1 step backward

Indefinite loop in code

Selection
Everyday condition-start-action
if not done enough work
    stay in to finish it

Selection
condition-start-action in algorithm
if hungry
    rub tummy

Condition-start-action in code

Selection
Everyday condition-switches-between-actions
if not done enough work
    stay in to finish it
else
    go out to play

Selection
In algorithm condition-switches-between-actions
if partner waves
    say "that was fun"
else
    Hum gently

Condition-switches-between-actions in code

Selection in a loop
algorithm
Loop always
    if touching red
    jump once

Selection in a loop in code

Basic Procedures
Everyday Dog Procedures
define roll_over
Lie on side
Lie on back
lie on side

Called by saying roll_over

Main Program
procedure

Basic Procedures in Code

define procedure
action
action
action
Procedure

Nested Loops
In algorithms
do 3 times
    jump
    do 4 times
    stand
    sit

Nested Loops In Code

Variables to store and change numbers in algorithms
Assign 3 to my_num
Hum for my_num seconds
Pause for my_num seconds
Loop my_num times
    jump
Add 2 to my_num
Say my_num

Placeholder Variables in Code
set name to Bob
Say join Hi name

Variables in algorithm
Assign Bob to name variable
Say Hi name
Say Boo name

Variables as placeholders
Everyday Variables Wedding Placenames

Variables to change numbers in code
set count to 0
repeat 10
Say count for 1 seconds
Change count by 1

Adaptable Procedures in Algorithm

define jump height
if key space pressed? then
change y by height
wait 1 seconds
Procedure

Adaptable Procedures in Code

when clicked
forever
jump 40
Main Program

Committed to Improvements

HIAS, Hampshire's Inspection & Advisory Service, is committed to developing and improving these resources. We recognize that primary programming is still its infancy in comparison with other subjects and that new research and primary practice will refine and improve teaching and learning in this area. All royalties earnt from this series will be used to write more computing books and revise these resources as needed.

Photocopiable resource for pupils

Teacher Hints & Tips on the same resource

INTRODUCING NEW CONCEPTS

Introducing Simple Sequence

These slides can be downloaded from https://computing.hias.hants.gov.uk/course/view.php?id=51.

Part One: Simple Sequence

They are designed to be delivered to the whole class before pupils move on to using simple sequence in any module of work in this book. If pupils have used the slides before a previous module of work omit them.

Part Two: Fast & Slow

Is designed to be delivered before the conversation or animation modules. If pupils have not viewed sequence or fast and slow, then deliver one in the first session and the second in a further lesson.

They can also be delivered to a small group of pupils if they are working independently through resources in pairs.

Format

Slides are provided in PDF and PowerPoint Formats and teachers who purchased the book are authorized to adapt the resources within their school or on closed learning platforms such as Seesaw, Google Classroom or Teams as long as they are not shared outside the school community.

Hints

Extra hints and tips on usage are provided alongside each slide on the following pages.

Resources

Pupils will need whiteboards and pens or paper and pencils.

Summary Sheet

These is a summary sheet that follows this slide commentary that pupils can use to write their algorithms on and be reminded about key knowledge.

Programming Concepts Simplified

Simple Sequence

©HIAS  Hampshire Services

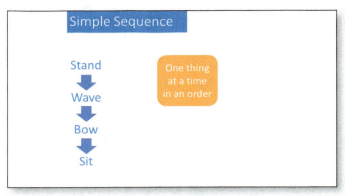

A simple definition of sequence. NOTE sequences can include other concepts such as repetition or selection but for this book these more complex ideas are omitted, hence simple sequence.

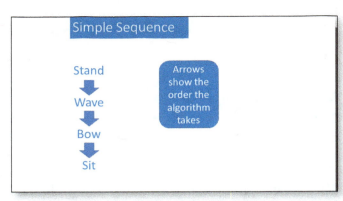

Point out that sequences start at the top and work there way down. They could also go from left to right. Pupils should know that an algorithm is a set of instructions to do something that can be understood by a human and you may want to remind them of this.

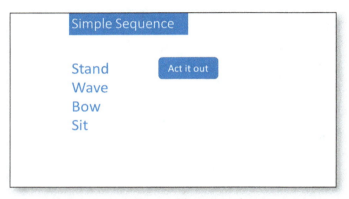

Ask pupils to act it out. You could point to the actions one at a time to help them.

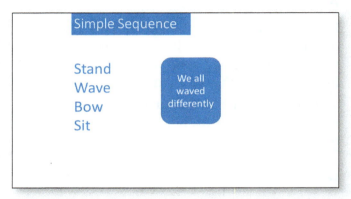

Point out that some people waved in different ways. This is fine as we have not given much detail.

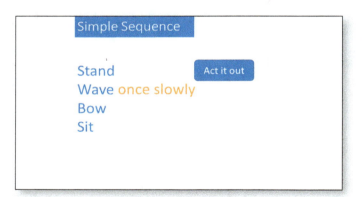

Ask pupils to act out this adapted algorithm.

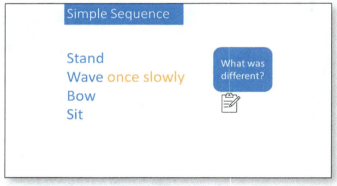

Ask them to either write down what is different or tell their neighbours.

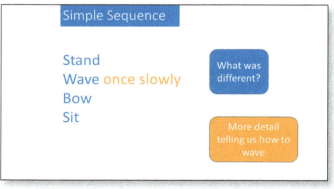

Accept any answers that point out that wave has more detail telling us how to wave

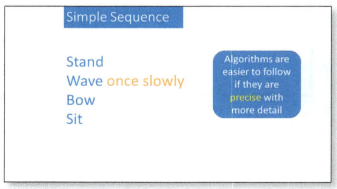

Read the slide and explain what precise it if any need this,

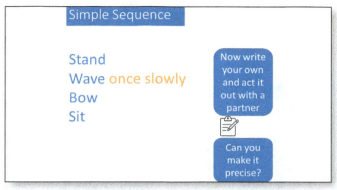

Instruct pupils to write their own algorithm and then give them to their neighbour to act out. They can have more actions. If any pupils struggled to act out the last algorithm check their work first. Offer to scribe for poor writers.

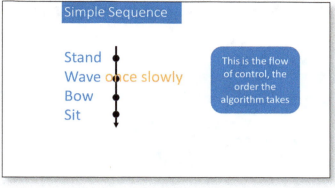

As you read through the algorithm, again point to the dots on the line. Explain that this is the flow of control, the order the instructions take in this algorithm.

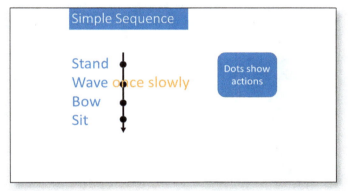

Dots show actions

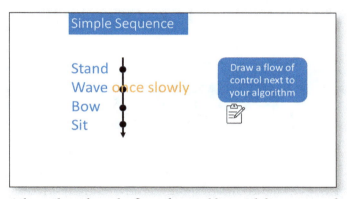

Ask pupils to draw the flow of control line and dots on top of their sequence algorithms.

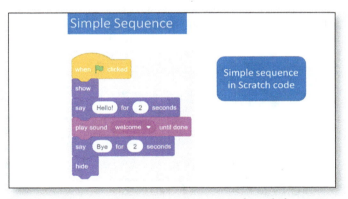

Point to the code blocks one at a time and read them. You could also explain what each command will do. Point out that they will be run in order from top to bottom.

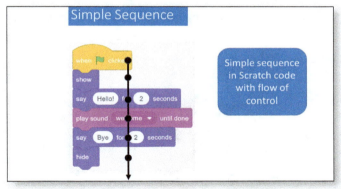

Programming has the same flow of control as the algorithm. From top to bottom.

(Part 2 is important in the conversation and animation modules.)

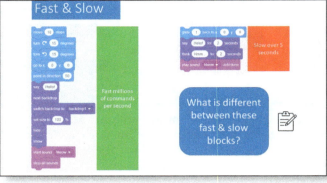

Here are some example fast and slow blocks. Can pupils either write down what is different about both groups or tell their neighbours.

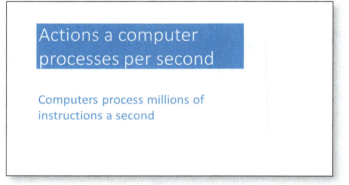

Process means act on. So computers carry out millions of instructions per second.

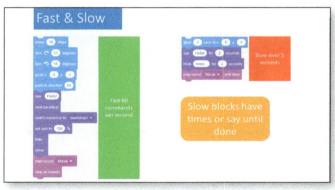

Make sure pupils understand that the slower blocks have built in timings and the fast blocks don't have timings.

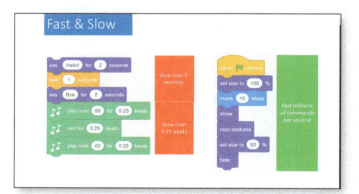

Blocks on the right run very fast, millions of instructions every second so all of these would happen in less than one second. Some might even be too quick to see. Blocks on the left are slower.

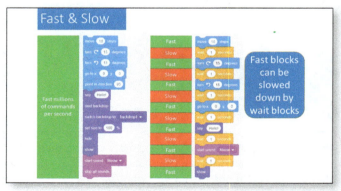

Point out how some of the fast blocks on the left have been slowed down on the right. You might even want to demo this directly in Scratch.

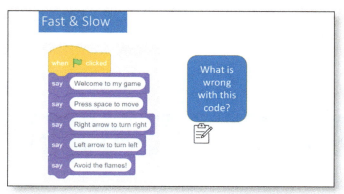

Ask pupils to either write down or tell their neighbour what is wrong with this code?

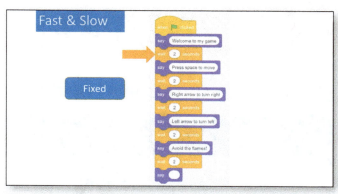

Here is one fix where the times have been added by using wait blocks to slow the code down. The empty block at the end stops the last speech block from continuing forever.

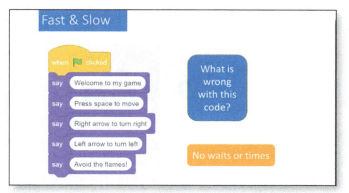

Read the answer in orange. Explain that when this is run, only the last block would be shown as the rest would whizz through at high speed.

Drag these out and show pupils what happens when they are run.

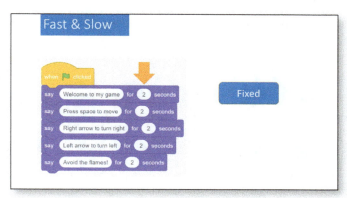

Here is another fix where say blocks with built in times have been used. Both solutions work well.

Timing Matters in Programming

Look out for blocks with built in times and blocks without

Finally a quick summary slide.

Humans are surrounded by digital devices

Digital devices are objects controlled by programming

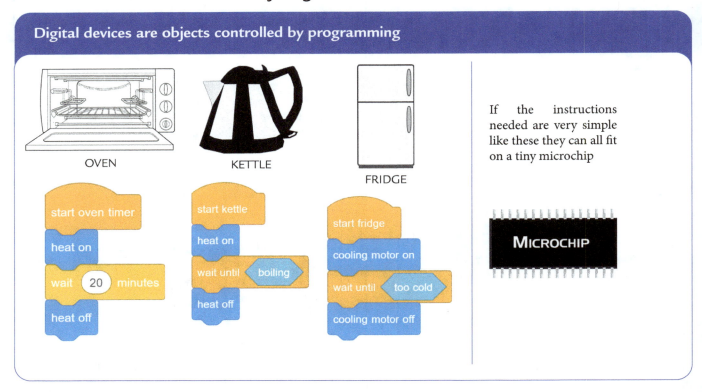

If the instructions needed are very simple like these they can all fit on a tiny microchip

Can you think of any other digital devices?

Computers are digital devices designed to run lots of programmes.

We can write new programmes using programming languages like Scratch.

We are learning about

Simple sequences

One instruction following another like the programming above.

Algorithms

A set of instructions or rules to do something.

Algorithms can be used to plan programs like this oven planning algorithm.

> Press a button
> Start the heat
> Wait 30 mins
> Turn the heat off

People use algorithms to plan all sorts of other non-programming things such as the best way to get to school or the best way to cook a cake.

We are also learning

How to control programming in Scratch using key board, mouse or trackpad **inputs**.

The power of waits to slow our programmes down

Inputs **put in** information into digital devices. Keyboard, trackpad and mouse are computer inputs. Buttons and dials are oven inputs.

photocopiable page

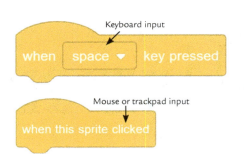

Keyboard input

Mouse or trackpad input

Everyday Sequence Algorithm

MODULES OF WORK

How this module fits into a programming progression

This is an introductory module designed to be used with primary pupils who have never used Scratch before. Its main aim is to help pupils familiarize themselves with the environment before going on to create more complex projects.

You start by introducing simple sequence using the slides on page 13 before decomposing a working game together as a class. You then build the game together, your pupils copying you to learn about Scratch functionality. Pupils tick off the key skills as they build the project with you. Finally they design and build their own game ticking off the Scratch skills they learned as they use them.

Things to do before you teach the project

- Know how you are going to access Scratch (online logged in, online logged out, offline, etc)
- Print out enough decompose the game worksheets (p. xx) for one each
- Print a decompose answer sheet for yourself
- Print a few support cards found on pages 31-34 in case some pupils need them
- Choose one of the skills list versions page 29 or 30 and print one for each child
- Print a planning sheet on page 26 for each child.

Resources

Animal Challenges online
https://scratch.mit.edu/projects/636084963/
Decompose worksheet and answer sheet
Planning Sheet
Skills list A or B

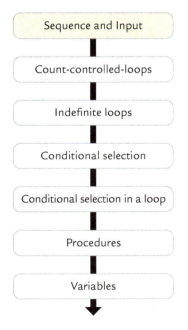

Sequence and Input

Count-controlled-loops

Indefinite loops

Conditional selection

Conditional selection in a loop

Procedures

Variables

Overview
1. Introduce simple sequence
2. Decompose the game
3. Explain the plan
4. Choose plan view animal sprite
5. Delete the ones you don't want to use
6. Rename the main animal sprite
7. Move   7A. Longer move from number keys
8. **EMERGENCY RETURN BUTTON**
9. Steering   9A. Experiment with degrees
10. Save or download a copy
11. Testing
12. Paint a cheese
13. Program the cheese   13A. Create other obstacles effects
14. Duplicate cheese with code inside
15. Code instructions
16. Create obstacle sprites challenge
17. Create background
18. Pupils design and build there own game

Pupils will need access to either

Scratch online with a Scratch login

Scratch online without a Scratch login

Offline Scratch 3

A PC, Mac or Chromebook

This module has **not** been designed for a tablet although an earlier version here was adapted for a tablet

http://code-it.co.uk/animalchallenges/

Methodologies

Decomposition (2)

I do you do (most)

Parsons (12)

Working individually (18)

You can find out more about these concepts from the teacher book

---

Learning Objectives

Blocks

I can link keys to commands

I can choose and place a programming block carefully

I can delete a programming block

Sprites

I can choose a sprite from the library

I can draw a simple sprite

I can duplicate (copy) a sprite

I can delete a sprite

I know that if you delete a sprite it deletes all its code

I can undelete a sprite

I can get my sprite back if it goes off the screen

Stage

I Know that the stage can have many backdrops (pictures)

I Know where the stage is

I can choose a new stage backdrop from library

I can draw my own backdrops

---

1. Introduce simple sequence

Use the slides and commentary simple sequence

2. Decompose the game

Open animal challenge on your interactive white board or touch screen TV in Scratch 3

Make the game full screen.

Give out the decomposition sheet and instruct pupils to match the instruction to what it does by drawing a line when they see it in action on the game.

Play the game starting it with a green flag.

Read the instructions out loud and play the game using the space bar to move forward and the left and right arrows to steer left and right.

Make sure pupils can see that you are pressing the space bar to move forward and the right and left arrows to steer.

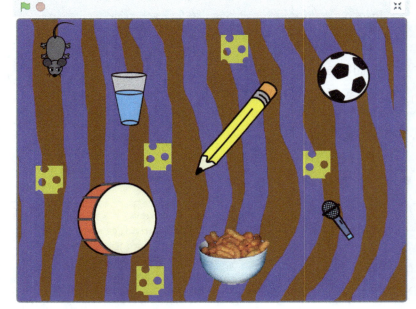

Animal Challenge Full Screen

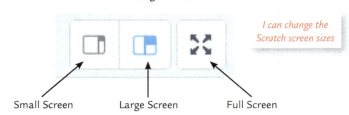

I can change the Scratch screen sizes

Small Screen   Large Screen   Full Screen

Exaggerate your key presses and say out loud what buttons you are pressing on the keyboard or what you are pressing on the screen.

When most pupils have completed the sheet, go through the answers together. There is an answer sheet to help you.

Explain that the green flag does many things. Can they spot what they are? You may need to play the game a few more times so they can observe the following events closely

- Send mouse back to the start
- Point mouse down
- Game instructions
- Show cheeses

3. Explain the plan

Explain that each pupil is going to make a similar game to the animal challenges although they might choose a different character and different obstacles. Along the way they are going to learn lots of things about Scratch programming. Give out the skills list for pupils to tick as you go.

4. Choose plan view animal sprites

Ask pupils to log on and start Scratch

Demonstrate how to choose a sprite from library

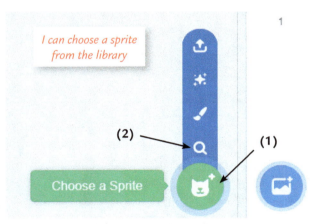

Choose Sprite from Library

Hover cursor over cat+ icon (1)

Move up to choose a sprite (2)

Choose animals tab at the top to just look for animals

Explain that plan view sprites are seen from above

If you move your cursor over the animal, it will cycle through all the costumes. If one of these is from above, it can be included.

Ask if anyone can see a sprite seen from above?

Answer Beetle, Cat2, Crab are early examples

Select one

Go through the process once more selecting a new plan view sprite

Now instruct pupils to find as many plan view animal sprites as they can

Give them time to do so

Formative Assessment Opportunities

Watch your pupils, if any are unable to do this demonstrate it again for them and record your support on their assessment sheet.

Are any pupil doing the work for their neighbour? If they are explain that they should not do this as they are not helping them but making their neighbour helpless. Ask them would they write a sum in their neighbours maths book or complete a sentence in their neighbour's writing book?

5. Delete the sprites you don't want to use

Show pupils how to delete a sprite

Left click on the dustbin on top right of selected sprite

Demonstrate how to delete a sprite again

Now instruct all pupils to delete all sprites but keep one that they want to keep as their main sprite. Pupils have to spend time finding sprites or they will do it later when you want them to concentrate on more important aspects of programming.

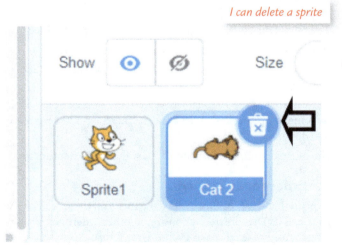

Delete Sprite

6. Rename the main animal sprite

Name is directly above sprites. Highlight and type a new name.

> **PROGRAMMING KNOWLEDGE**
>
> Naming objects in programming is important as some code will refer directly to the name. When your project has lots of objects a bad name such as sprite 1 will not help pupils find the object which will slow down debugging.

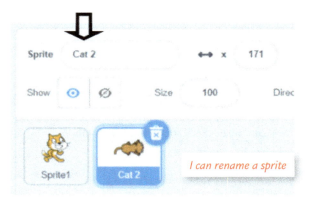

I can rename a sprite

Rename Sprite

7. Move

Explain that you are now going to provide the programming to make their sprite move.

Make sure you are on your sprite and not the backdrop.

The sprite shows a blue halo around it when it is selected.

You can also see a picture of your sprite in the top right corner of the coding area. Point these out to pupils.

Drag out a ***when space key is pressed*** starting block from events.

Show pupils how the arrow head can be used to open a menu and select other keys although in this case the space key is the right one.

Navigate to the motion commands and ask the pupils which block might help them move once the space key is pressed.

Drag out the move 10 steps and hold it just underneath the when space key pressed block, a grey shadow will appear showing that the blocks will soon be linked.

Selected Sprite with Blue Halo

7A. Move further extension with number keys

Pupils who finish quickly can create new blocks where number keys move further such as when two key is pressed move 20 steps.

Tell pupils that this is the snap to shadow or snap to line.

It helps you know where you are placing something.

Make sure you demonstrate this slowly as pupils make lots of mistakes by just snapping blocks too quickly.

Explain that move 10 means move 10 tiny dots of pixels. Pixel dots make up the screen. In Scratch, there are 420 across and 380 down.

Now instruct pupils to create and test their move command.

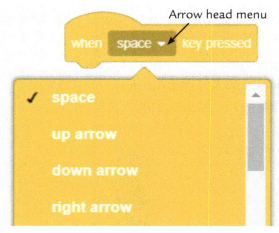

Drop Down Menu

8. Emergency return

Explain that it is possible to move the sprite off the screen so you can't see it. Demonstrate choosing another when key pressed sprite and dropping down to find r for return. Then snap a go to x and y block and change the number code to 0 0 as shown. Explain that these blocks position code in different places on the screen and 0 0 is the centre of the screen. Then add a show block from the looks menu just in case the sprite has been hidden. Now move the sprite away and test the r key. Does it return to the centre if it does you have made an emergency return.

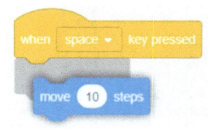

Snap to Shadow

> **SUPPORT**
>
> There is card with these blocks on that you can print to help anyone who needs more than your demonstration

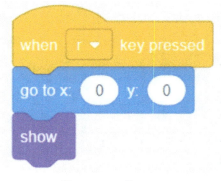

Emergency Return

9. Steering

Explain that they are now going to provide the code to make their animal turn right or left.

Drag out two when key pressed blocks.

Demonstrate changing these to right and left arrow.

Go to the motion blocks and ask pupils which blocks might be useful?

Challenge them to find the right blocks to make the right arrow on the keyboard turn right and the left arrow on the keyboard turn left. Remind them of the decomposition exercise earlier.

9A. Experiment with degrees

Encourage pupils to try different amounts of turn between 5 and 90 degrees.

Remind them to make both right and left turns the same.

10. Save or download a copy

Of course this may need to be done earlier or later depending on the speed of your sessions. Regular saving is always to be encouraged as well as incrementing each save by adding the next number in the series. af1 af2, etc.

If you are using Scratch 3 online and logged on

File and **save now** although projects will be automatically saved even if pupils forget.

If you are using Scratch 3 online but not logged in

File and **save to your computer**

This file must them be found and moved to pupil home areas as it will automatically go to the downloads area. See the fix on the right for a better solution.

If you are using Scratch 3 offline editor

File and **save to your computer**

Save in normal windows or Mac way

11. Testing

After each code build pupils should always test what they have built to see if it works. Some pupils will need you to remind them.

12. Paint a cheese

Demonstrate how pupils can draw their own cheeses.

1. Hover over the new sprite icon and then move up to select paint.
2. Choose the rectangle tool.
3. Change the fill colour to a cheese appropriate yellow.
4. Remove the outline (red diagonal line from selection tools).
5. Drag out a square, making sure it is centred across the reticule in the centre of the screen. This is the rotate point of a sprite which will not be important for this project but may be important in the future.

Then use the eraser tool to remove some holes.

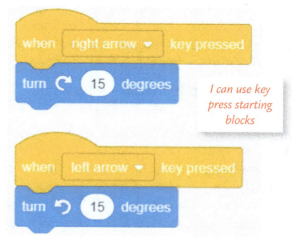

I can use key press starting blocks

Steering blocks

I can change a block to make it act differently

Saving if using Scratch online but not logged in

Both Chrome and the Edge have a setting change that allows pupils to choose where they save downloads. Your network administrator will be able to set these up remotely and apply them as a policy for all pupils in your school. This makes using Scratch without logging in much easier.

I can save a copy of my work regularly

Paint New Sprite

Rectangle Tool   Fill   Outline   Selection Tools

Reticule

SUPPORT

There is a card with the paint blocks on to help any that struggle but a good demo will work for most pupils

Instruct pupils that they don't have to create chesses but it must be a simple shape using the circle or rectangle tool.

Give them time to create a couple of sprites before choosing the best one to use in the game.

13. Program the cheese

Make sure your chosen sprite is selected.

Sprite picture in top right of coding window.

Blue halo around the sprite.

Drag out when green flag clicked, show, hide, wait until & touching blocks

Change the touching block to the name of your main character.

Show pupils how the touching mighty mouse can fit inside the wait until.

Point out that the shapes give a clue that they will work together.

Remind pupils that when they decomposed the game the green flag made the cheeses show if they were hidden and then once the mouse touched them they disappeared.

Give pupils time to experiment with the order and test it.

Instruct them not to copy from their neighbour and that it is fine to try an order that doesn't work as you learn something from this.

Formative Assessment Opportunities

Watch pupils do this. Record any pupil who does this quickly and any who persevere but gets there independently.

Show pupils the correct solution before you move on.

14. Duplicate cheese with code inside

Once pupils have created and tested their code they are ready to duplicate the spite and spread them around the screen.

Right mouse click on the sprite tile and select duplicate.

All the code will also be duplicated.

The cheese sprites can then be spread around the screen evenly.

15. Code instructions

The technical name for our first three blocks of code under the green flag is initialization. Initialization code makes sure that the program always runs the same way every time the program is run.

Make sure you are inside the main animal sprite character by checking the image in the top left-hand side of the coding area and the blue halo around the sprite tile.

Drag out the code as shown on the right a block as a time and get pupils to build it and experiment with it before moving on.

Encourage pupils to experiment with the set size to % block as this can aid their mathematical understanding.

Before they drag out the go to x and y block, ask pupils to move their sprite to where they would like it to start on the screen. Explain that when the x and y block is dragged out it remembers the position of the sprite when it is added. If pupils have not encountered cartesian coordinates yet don't go any further.

The point in direction block can be adapted for all angles. It has a draggable dial if the number is selected.

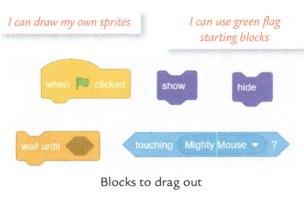

I can draw my own sprites

I can use green flag starting blocks

Blocks to drag out

I can use wait until blocks

Correct Solution

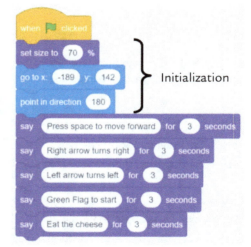

I can make a copy of a sprite and its code

Duplicate a Sprite

Initialization

I know that initiation code makes the sprite run the same every time it is run

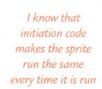

Direction Number Dial

16. Create obstacle sprites

Challenge pupils to import obstacles to spread around their screen.

Obstacles can't hide or they might be mistaken for things to be collected but they could do other things when they are touched such as say something or make a sound.

What effects can pupils create that happen when the main character touches the obstacles?

Give pupils plenty of time to create these

Formative assessment opportunities

This is a great opportunity to observe pupils and see who can adapt what they have learnt in a similar but different context.

It fits in with.

You can create something that is similar but not the same as any examples I provided on the assessment sheet.

17. Create background

This is a great opportunity to draw a colourful background.

Left click on the stage icon (bottom right).

Select the paint icon as shown on the right.

Make sure you are on bitmap mode and use the drawing tools.

18. Plan and build your own game

In this section, pupils plan their own similar project and then build it ticking off the key skills as they go. There is space for them to write there own skills discovered at the bottom. There is also an alternative tick sheet where they can say if the idea was their own or another pupil in the class. My thanks to Cobie van de Ven @hetdiglab for this adaptation.

There is a simple 10-minute planner to complete first.

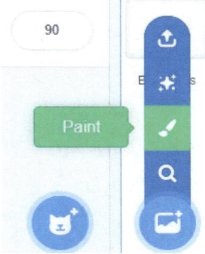

I can draw a Scratch backdrop

Stage Options

MY GAME PLANNER

To go with
Section 18

Ideas Level

My character _____ will move about and be steered through an obstacle course of

_____ . When my character touches the obstacles, they will _____

_____.

Design Level

Draw the game layout. Mark in where your characters will start

photocopiable page

Commands

Press space key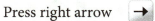

Press right arrow

Touched by mighty mouse

Press left arrow ←

Mighty Mouse

move forward

turn right

turn left

Cheese
Disappear

> Game Worksheet
> to go with Section 1

- -

Commands

Press space key

Press right arrow →

Touched by mighty mouse

Press left arrow ←

Mighty Mouse

move forward

turn right

turn left

Cheese
Disappear

> Game Worksheet
> to go with Section 1

photocopiable page

Animal Challenges – Page 27

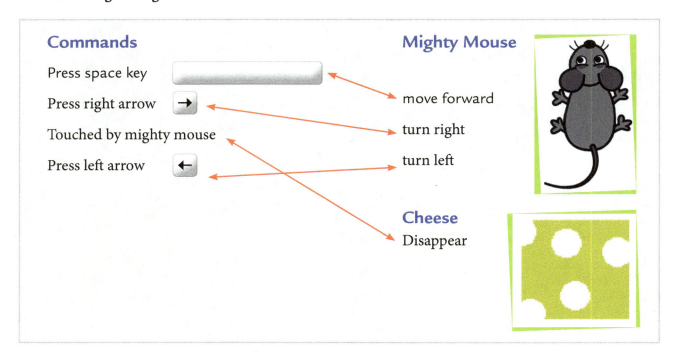

Animal Challenges Pupil Skills Checklist Version A Name: _____

Learning Objectives	With teacher	On my own
I can change the Scratch screen sizes		
I can choose a sprite from the library		
I can delete a sprite		
I can rename a sprite		
I can join Scratch blocks together		
I can use key press starting blocks		
I can change a block to make it act differently		
I can save a copy of my work regularly		
I can draw my own sprites		
I can use green flag starting blocks		
I can use wait until blocks		
I can make a copy of a sprite and its code (duplicate)		
I know that initiation code makes the sprite run the same every time it is run		
I can draw a Scratch backdrop		
I can plan a similar Scratch project		
I know that if I delete a sprite, it deletes all the code as well		
I can undelete a sprite		
Other skills I have learned	■	■
	■	
	■	
	■	
	■	

Animal Challenges Pupil Skills Checklist Version B   Name: _____

Learning Objectives	With teacher	On my own
I can change the Scratch screen sizes		
I can choose a sprite from the library		
I can delete a sprite		
I can rename a sprite		
I can join Scratch blocks together		
I can use key press starting blocks		
I can change a block to make it act differently		
I can save a copy of my work regularly		
I can draw my own sprites		
I can use green flag starting blocks		
I can use wait until blocks		
I can make a copy of a sprite and its code (duplicate)		
I know that initiation code makes the sprite run the same every time it is run		
I can draw a Scratch backdrop		
I can plan a similar Scratch project		
I know that if I delete a sprite, it deletes all the code as well		
I can undelete a sprite		

New Skill I Have Learnt	Who I learnt it from, name or self	

photocopiable page

Move

and

Steer

Back

Move And Steer

Emergency Return

Support Card

Back

Build an

Emergency

Return

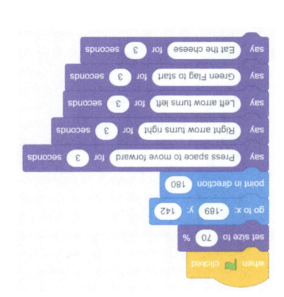

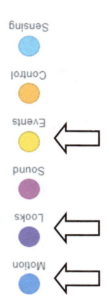

Instructions

Instructions

Back

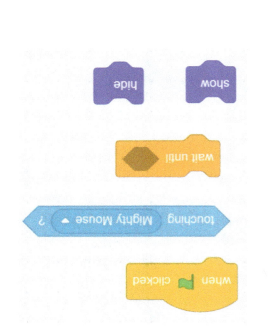

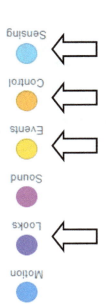

Wait Until Touching
Sprite
Parsons
Back

Wait Until

Touching

Sprite

Parsons

Module Aims: Pupils learn about simple sequence away from computers. Pupils build simple monologues using parsons methodology. Pupils design and program a conversation between two characters using a cross-curricular theme chosen by their teacher or them.

Cross-Curricular Focus

The basic conversation premise can be adapted for use across all areas of the curriculum. It could be a dentist explaining dental hygiene techniques or a pair of stone age characters talking about their new tools. A powerful farewell at a train station as part of a WW2 evacuation scene or a campaigner trying to persuade a shopkeeper to stock Fairtrade produce.

Things to do before teaching the module

- Print out Monologue algorithms to go with parsons section
- Make sure your pupils can access Monologue Programming
- Scratch Template file
- Download sequence slides
- Print out two character algorithm planner for each pupil
- Optionally print out three person planner for pupils who need higher challenge
- Print out conversation knowledge assessment this has two assessment per page so cut page in half

Online Resources

Scratch Monologue Programming

https://scratch.mit.edu/projects/636625538/

Sequence slides part A can be found here xxxx

Fast & Slow Blocks Part B can be found here xxxxx

How this module fits into a programming progression

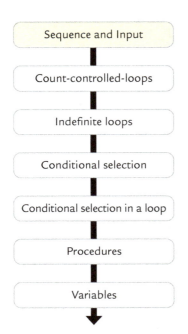

Sequence of learning

1. Introduce the concept of simple sequence and fast and slow blocks using the slides found on pages x and x
2. Parsons monologues
3. Introduce your chosen conversation hook
4. Model taking part in a conversation
5. Model writing a conversation with waits
6. Pupils write a conversation algorithm
7. Model turning your algorithm into code
8. Pupils turn their algorithms into code
9. Extension ideas
10. True and False Knowledge Assessment

Programming Concepts

- Sequence

National Curriculum Programs of Study

Pupils should be taught to:

- **design, write and debug programs that accomplish specific goals,** including controlling or simulating physical systems; solve problems by decomposing them into smaller parts
- **use sequence,** selection and repetition **in programs;** work with variables and **various forms of input and output**
- **use logical reasoning** to explain how some simple algorithms work and **to detect and correct errors in algorithms and programs**

Key Sequence Knowledge
The order actions or instructions are arranged in is a sequence

Algorithmic Knowledge
I can make my instructions more precise so that they are more likely to be followed exactly as I wanted them to be

I can finish my instructions so no one will be in doubt as to what they do

When planning an algorithm that will be converted into code I will consider what type of instructions can be turned into code and use these

Programming Knowledge
I am careful to order my sequence as I know that the same blocks ordered in a different way will produce different outcomes

I can include wait commands in sequences to slow down the speed that blocks without timings are run in Scratch

I can choose a way to start my sequence that might involve a keyboard, mouse or trackpad input so they can be run

Types of knowledge Key

Declarative knowledge
Static facts or knowledge stored in your memory

Procedural knowledge
How to perform a specific skill or task

Conditional Knowledge
When to use declarative and procedural knowledge

1. Introduce the concept of simple sequence

Use the slides to introduce simple sequence if you have not used these before. Pupils will need either the knowledge organiser sheet found on page 18 to record their own simple sequence algorithm or a whiteboard and a pen. At some point, introduce Fast & slow blocks part B using slides this works well as a second lesson intro.

2. Parsons monologue

Ask pupils to use the monologue algorithm planning sheet to build the monologues programs in Scratch. The Churchill and Julius Caesar sprites use timed blocks while Tables and Victorian child use blocks without built in times. Scratch blocks separate into those that run very quickly and those that have built in timing that finish once their time is up. It is worth exploring how these work.

Pupils will need access to Scratch and the template Monologue Programming found here https://scratch.mit.edu/projects/636625538/

	No timer	Timer
Auto end	No	Yes after the time
Move straight to next block	Yes	No wait for timer to finish

3. Share the hook

Take a few moments to excite and enthuse your pupils about the conversation hook you or they have chosen.

4. Model taking part in a conversation

Write WAIT in large letters on two whiteboards. Hand one to a child or adult helper and keep the other one yourself. Have a very simple conversation about something you both know about. When you are speaking, the child should hold up wait. When they are speaking you hold up wait. Explain that they are waiting for the same time that you are talking and visa versa.

5. Model writing a conversation with waits

Model a conversation opener that links to your theme on your interactive board. It could end up looking something like this shown below.

6. Pupils write a conversation algorithm

Give pupils time to complete their conversation algorithm on the algorithm planning sheet provided on page 41.

Give everyone at least 5 minutes before you start checking their work.

Formative Assessment Support

Start with your learners who struggle with writing the most as they are the most likely to make errors in this algorithm. On the first scan of the classes work, look for zig-zag pattern as the conversation moves from side to side down the page. On the second scan look for times that are the same on each line as the wait of one character matches the speech of another. On the third scan look for good ideas that you can praise and others can magpie or adapt.

Corrective activity

Take your wait white boards with you and model their speech and waits to point out where two people are talking at the same time for the same length of time. Be sure to emphasize where one character is out of synch with the others due to different timings. Check back to make sure they correct this.

With very slow writers be willing to scribe the latter part of their conversation as long as they tell you exactly where to write it and how long to say it for.

Enrichment activity

A particularly literate child could be encouraged to adapt their conversation algorithm to include three people. There is a three character extension planner at the end of the chapter.

Can they bring in a third character and continue their conversation on the three character sheet?

I would only recommend this for pupils working far above the level of the rest of the class.

Character 1 Modern Girl	Time secs	Character 2 Viking Boy	Time secs
Do your parents know you have that sharp knife?	3	Wait	3
Wait	3 / Total Time	All the children in our village carry knives apart from the slaves.	3 / Total Time
You have slaves, that is so wrong!	3 / Total Time	Wait	3 / Total Time

Zig Zag

7. Modelling turning your algorithm into code

Import two sprites using the choose a sprite button. Encourage pupils to choose ones that move when they hover over them as this different positions could be chosen as part of the conversation.

Add a when green flag clicked starting block to each sprite from the light yellow events side button and ask the pupils where the green flag is run on the screen? Top middle to the right.

Drag out a say hello for two seconds block and a wait block and start to turn your algorithm into code. Frequently refer back to your conversation modelled earlier and make a great play over matching the times and order of the conversation to the algorithm. At this point, do not add any animations or background changes.

8. Pupils turn their algorithms into code

Give pupils plenty of time to turn their algorithms into code. If possible, allow pupils to work independently as soon as you have checked their algorithm plan.

Evaluating Programming 10/15 minutes into the session ask pupils to talk to their neighbours and discuss what criteria they will use to determine if their program works. Draw out that the conversation will make sense. That one character will talk while another will listen. That there will be enough time to read the speech bubbles but not so much time that the reader gets bored. That the subject matter will be interesting and engage the reader.

Debugging conversation problems

Instruct pupils to go back to their algorithm line by line working their way through one character first and check their code is the same as the algorithm.

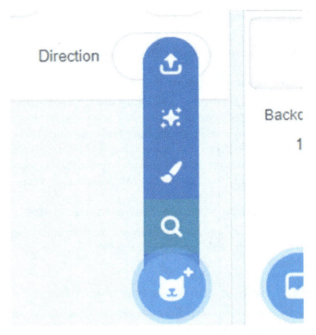

Choose a sprite button

Improving writing

Use literacy knowledge of the pupil to appropriately challenge/support them to improve their writing.

Evaluation criteria

Do the characters talk at different times?

Does the speech make sense?

Is the speech interesting and engaging?

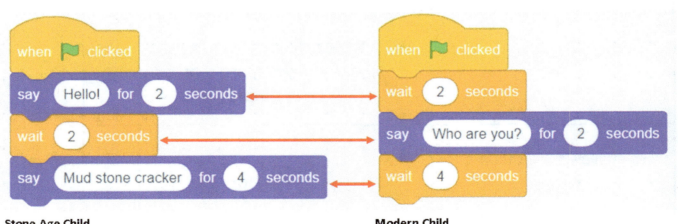

Stone Age Child   **Modern Child**

9. Extension ideas

In these sections, you introduce pupils to a few ideas and encourage them to experiment to discover new ideas for themselves. Before you start you get pupils to complete the time+ column on their algorithm planning sheet by adding up the times as they go down the algorithm planner. You also explain that the extras column can be used to plan where different effects will happen. When you demonstrate how backgrounds and facing can be changed, make sure you plan this on your algorithm sheet extras column first.

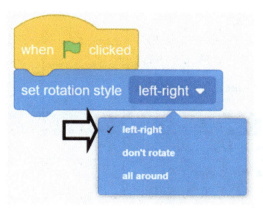

Facing left and right

Facing

In a natural conversation, characters look away occasionally. Scratch can program that as well.

First set the character to left and right only using set rotation to left and right. Now you can use point in direction blocks to face right or left after a time period.

This can be created in its own separate script with its own starting block as shown on the right or built into the existing speech code.

Now you can build up a script using waits informed by time+ column and point in direction blocks.

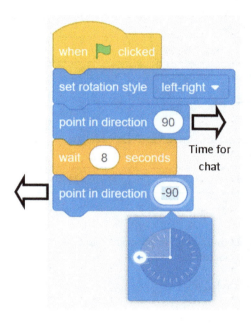

Time for chat

Initialization

Code like set rotation style and the first point in direction is initialization code designed to make the sprite act in the same way every time.

Change backgrounds

Show pupils how they can import a background.

Stage button bottom right

Choose a backdrop

Point out the names and show pupils where they can rename them.

Stage

Backdrop tab

Costume name

You may also wish to demonstrate how a background can be changed after a period of time through the use of a script.

Similar to the facing one informed by the time+ timings

Choose a backdrop

Summative conversation assessment criteria

• Do the characters talk at different times?

• Does the speech make sense?

• Is the speech interesting and engaging?

10. True and false knowledge assessment

There is an optional knowledge assessment sheet for you to use if you wish

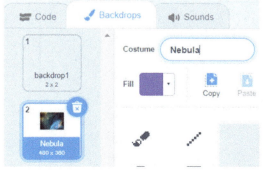

Renaming a background

Churchill Idea

Change the Scratch cat to look like Winston Churchill and then make it say one of his speeches.

Churchill Speech Algorithm

Speech	Seconds
We shall fight on the seas and oceans.	3
We shall fight with growing confidence and growing strength in the air.	4
We shall defend our Island.	2
Whatever the cost may be.	2
We shall fight on the beaches.	2
We shall fight on the landing grounds.	3
We shall fight in the fields and in the streets.	3
We shall fight in the hills.	2
We shall never surrender.	2

Caesar Idea

Make a Julius Caesar character and program it to say one of his speeches about the people of Britain.

Caesar Speech algorithm

Julius Caesar on Britons written in 53BCE for propaganda purposes (translated from Latin)

Speech	Seconds
Start when clicked	
All the Britons,	2
dye themselves with woad,	3
which is a bluish colour.	3
This makes them look more terrible appearance in a fight	5
They wear their hair long	3
and have every part of their body shaved.	4
except their head and upper lip.	3

Victorian Child Idea

Choose a Victorian child character and program it to tell the audience about how it was like to work as a child.

Victorian Child Speech algorithm

Speech
Start when clicked
We work very long hours.
3 seconds
We have few breaks.
3 seconds
It can be very dangerous!
4 seconds
Some of us get hurt and die!
4 seconds
I was very young when I started work.
5 seconds
We don't go to school.
3 seconds
No speech

Tables Idea

Choose a character and program it to say the three times tables to help me learn them.

Tables Algorithm

1x3=3	2 seconds
2 seconds	8x3=24
2x3=6	2 seconds
2 seconds	9x3=27
3x3=9	2 seconds
2 seconds	10x3=30
4x3=12	2 seconds
2 seconds	11x3=33
5x3=15	2 seconds
2 seconds	12x3=36
6x3=18	2 seconds
2 seconds	Say nothing
7x3=21	

Character 1	Time secs	Character 2	Time secs	Extras	Time	Time+

Two character Algorithm Planner

photocopiable page

Character 1	Time secs	Character 2	Time secs	Character 3	Time secs	Extras	Time	Time+

Three character Algorithm Planner Extension

Conversation Knowledge Assessment

TRUE or FALSE

1. **Algorithms** are a way of planning programming

2. This block has its own built in timer

3. This block has its own built in timer

4. This block is an input block as it puts in information from the user

5. This block outputs information on to the screen for you to read

6. This code would be easy to read when it is run

Conversation Knowledge Assessment

TRUE or FALSE

1. **Algorithms** are a way of planning programming

2. This block has its own built in timer

3. This block has its own built in timer

4. This block is an input block as it puts in information from the user

5. This block outputs information on to the screen for you to read

6. This code would be easy to read when it is run

Conversation Knowledge Assessment – Page 43

TRUE or FALSE

1. **Algorithms** are a way of planning programming   TRUE (1 mark)

2. This block has its own built in timer   FALSE (1 mark)

3. This block has its own built in timer      TRUE (1 mark)

4. This block is an input block as it puts in information from the user
   TRUE (1 mark)

5. This block outputs information on to the screen for you to read
   TRUE (1 mark)

6. This code would be easy to read when it is run
   FALSE (1 mark)
   you would only be able to read the last line as the other blocks
   would run too fast.

CHAPTER 5   Fish Fun

Program Aim: Learn how to decompose and problem solve by programming a fun fish game. Steering the Carp to food without getting trapped in the lily pads.

Programming concepts
- Sequence
- Inputs

How this module fits into a programming progression

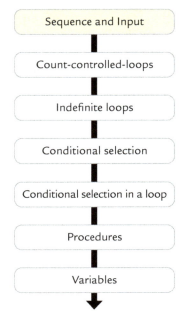

Sequence and Input

Count-controlled-loops

Indefinite loops

Conditional selection

Conditional selection in a loop

Procedures

Variables

Methodologies
Decomposition (2)
I do you do (most)
Parsons (12)
Working individually (18)

You can find out more about these concepts from the teacher book

National Curriculum Programs of Study
Pupils should be taught to:
- **design, write and debug programs that accomplish specific goals**, including controlling or simulating physical systems; **solve problems by decomposing them into smaller parts**
- **use sequence**, selection, and repetition **in programs**; work with variables and **various forms of input and output**
- **use logical reasoning** to explain how some simple algorithms work and **to detect and correct errors in algorithms and programs**

Things to do before the lesson
Download or link to Fish Fun https://scratch.mit.edu/projects/656042662/
Download the carp sprite if you intend to create the project exactly.
Print out the Decomposition sheet on page x one per pupil.
Follow the instructions to build your own version of fish fun first especially if you have not used Scratch before.
Print out a few copies of the support cards for pupils who need more time or have missed part of the lesson.

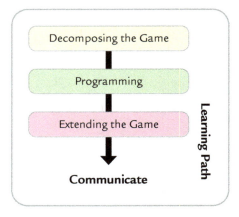

Cross-Curricular Focus
This can be adapted to fit in with many topics or projects. It could be a lost cave dweller trying to find their way home without falling from the rock walkway, a bee that has to pollenate each flower or a spaceship that has to visit every planet.

Methodologies used: *I do you do* to introduce basic block handling with simple sequences in Scratch. Parsons problems to construct working sequences in Sections 12 & 14. You can find out more about these strategies in the accompanying teacher work book.

Computational thinking
- Algorithmic thinking
- Decomposition

1. Objective & overview

Explain to pupils that they are going to decompose a game by playing it and working out what keys and game actions control which game actions.

After they have done this, the class is going to build the basics game together before adapting and improving it.

Explain that **decompose** means to break a problem up into parts and solve each part separately. Make this a part of your weekly vocabulary.

2. Decomposing the game

Either demo the game as a whole class or give pupils the link so they can try it themselves. Give them time to play it a few times. Don't allow them to look at the code to start with by using the full screen mode button. After 5–10 minutes of game play time, instruct pupils to fill in the decomposition sheet listing all the objects that they will need to make and circling in pencil all the things that the game does. You may wish to read these out to the class one by one to speed the process up and help poorer readers. Go through their answers using the marking sheet found on page x.

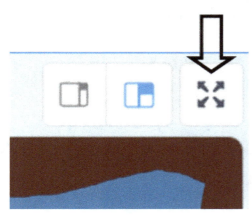

Full Screen Mode

3. Choose a starting point and justifying their choice

Ask pupils to decide where they think the best place to start creating the game would be. Get them to discuss it with their neighbours and mark their most important place as a 1 next to the task, 2 for the next most important, etc. Can they justify their choice to their friends? You are looking for answers that have clearly considered criteria such as the instructions as *no one will know how to pay the game* or carpet moving and steering as *there is nothing to do otherwise*. Prioritizing is a key part of coping with complexity which is important for decomposition, abstraction and all project management.

4. Links between algorithm and code

As you create the game, refer back to their decomposition sheet and get them to tick off aspects of the program they have created. In this way, you are helping to reinforce the connection between an algorithm plan and code.

Uploading the Carp Sprite From Network

5. Carp sprite

If you are making an exact copy of the game demonstrate uploading the carp sprite. This is a custom-made sprite not found in the game so make sure you have downloaded before the lesson and placed it somewhere on the network for pupils to access. Alternatively start with the carp only version. If pupils are going to choose their own main sprite, choose a sprite and demo looking for one that is viewed from above. Hover over the sprite to see if it has more than one costume (hint it moves).

Choose a sprite rather than using Carp

6. Move 10 steps when press the 1 key

Explain that they are going to start by making the main sprite move when they press the 1 key board input. (It is called an input because it puts information into the computer.) Explain that Scratch uses starting blocks which are curved. They can find these in events. Demonstrate how the arrow opens a drop down menu where they can link any key board input to their program.

Can they find a move block? Where might it be? Motion blocks. Drag out the move 10 steps and hold it so pupils can see the snap to line. Be slow and deliberate and they will too. Get them all to read the code out loud. Demonstrate how it works by pressing the 1 key. Can they do the same?

Starting Blocks Keys

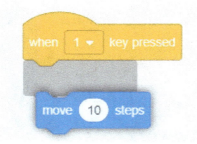

Snap to line

7. Move 20 steps when press the 2 key

Can pupils work out for themselves how to make a new section of code where the 2 key moves 20 steps?

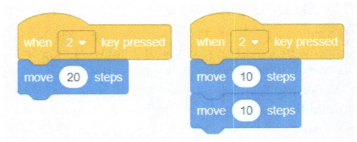

Two Possible Methods For Making 2 key
Move 20 Steps

Once they have experimented demonstrate both methods as shown above. You may wish to explain that the first is more elegant as it uses less code but both are correct.

8. Move backwards 10 steps when 0 key is pressed

Challenge pupils to discover how to make the main sprite move backwards 10 steps when the 0 key is pressed. Explain that this must be created in a new code section unconnected to previous code.

A good hint for this is to explain that there is an invisible + sign in front of the 10 then say I wonder what the inverse of add is?

Demonstrate the correct answer for any pupils that have not discovered it.

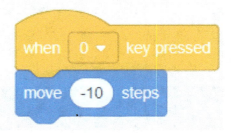

Backwards 10 steps

9. Pen commands

Explain that we now need to create the pen line that draws underneath the carp.

- Leave a trail when fish moves
- Stop leaving a trail when the u key is pressed
- Clear all lines when the e key is pressed

Drag out three when key is pressed blocks.

Then go to the add extension block (bottom left).

Explain that this adds extra pen blocks and that once they are added we can get to them through the menu on the far left.

Add Extension Button

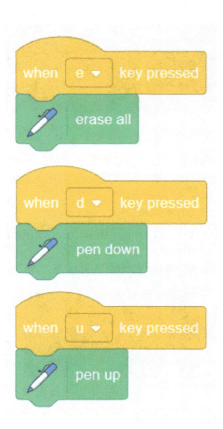

Costume Tab

Now drag out.

Erase all, pen down & pen up.

Snap each one on a separate **when key is pressed** block as shown.

Ask pupils if it would be alright if they all start with the same key?

You want them to identify that pen down and pen up would cancel each other out if they were controlled by the same key.

Ask them for key suggestions that will help them remember the key chosen. We have gone with first letter for the most significant word.

Change the letters to the one demonstrated and then ask them to create this code as shown on left.

10. Change costume

• Fish swims side to side when 1 or 2 key pressed

Select the Carp and open the costume tab.

Point out how there are two costumes (picture of the Carp) one flipping right and one flipping left. Click on them to show this. Explain that we can program the fish to change costumes in two ways.

Go back to the code and look inside the Looks blocks.

Point out the **switch costume to** block and menu drop down to show we can program each costume directly.

Then drag out the next costume block and combine it with a when key is pressed block but change it to any key. This means that the fish will look like it is swimming when any key is pressed.

Give pupils time to create and test this.

Carp Costumes

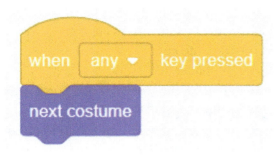

11. Backdrops

Create a backdrop

Click on stage and then click on backdrops.

Make sure you are in vector mode. It should say convert to bitmap at the bottom if you are in vector mode.

Select the brush tool.

Make the brush size 100.

Brush Size 100

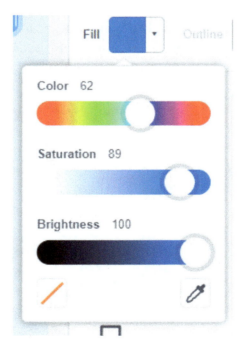

Change Colour

Start by selecting a dark blue colour.

Now use brush to draw across the whole screen. Do not worry if you go over the edge.

Give pupils time to create their own.

Now change the colour to brown for the edge and draw an edge.

Make sure only part of the pen ends up on the screen rectangle.

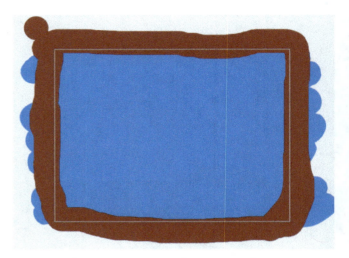

Give pupils time to create their own edge.

Now show pupils how to add a start position using the text tool and light colour. Corners work well for this. You may want to point out that the text manipulation box can be moved, resized and rotated.

Give pupils time to create their own starting point.

Text Manipulation Box

Duplicating backdrops

Right click on the backdrop to duplicate it. Do this twice.

Give pupils time to duplicate their backdrops.

Duplicate Backdrops

Explain that they are duplicating their backdrops because the fish fun example had different backdrops where the lily pads were in different places. Now we have all the background, edge and start we can copy it and add the lily pads.

Drawing lily pads

The easiest way to do this is to create a large green brush and paint three overlapping dots.

Three Overlapping Dots

Remind pupils that they must leave a path to the end.

Give pupils time to draw lily pads on every backdrop in different places.

12. Coding the stage to change

The easiest way to make the stage change is to create a green flag block and link it to next costume. If pupils have not used a green flag block before explain that it is a great starting block to use if you want many things to start at the same time.

Give pupils time to code and test this.

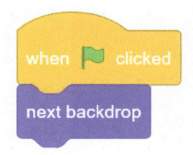

Coding the backdrops to change

13. Initialization code

Initialization is code that makes sure the program works in the same way every time. This often means clearing away the effects of the last program as well as returning sprites to the starting place.

Washing up and clearing the table is dinner initialization.

It would be difficult to eat your food if you have no clean plates to eat it from.

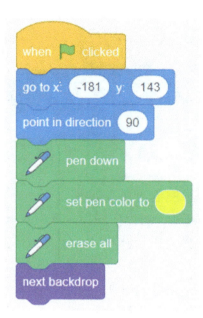

Tidying up the classroom and putting books away is lesson initialization.

It would be harder in the next lesson if the last lesson books are all left out to get in the way.

Add more code to the existing Green flag Block

As you do explain that the x and y blocks send objects to a specific place on a screen. They will be learning about this more in maths in year 5 or 6.

Drag the Carp sprite to the starting word.

Drag out a go to x and y blocks

Point in Direction Dial

This number has now been set to return to that place.

Move the sprite away and then green flag to test it.

Ask pupils to do the same.

Now drag out a point in direction block and click on the number to bring up the dial. Move the dial to point the sprite into the game.

Give them time to do the same.

Add pen down block

Explain that we want the pen to start down on the screen drawing so it will start drawing straight away.

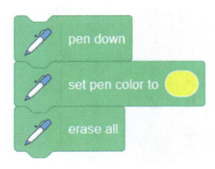

Add set pen colour to yellow

Explain that we want the line colour to show up against a yellow background.

Add erase all block

Explain that we want all the previous lines to vanish.

Finally remind pupils that the next backdrop created before also needs to be on the bottom so that everyone gets a new challenge when they start the game.

Explain that the order is important. If you swap positions for erase all and go to x and y blocks see what happens. You will need to play twice to spot the problem.

14. Coding the end

Say thing when touching Fish Food

Choosing and Ending Sprite

Choose a sprite

Find the Cheesy Puffs sprite

Shrink it to 20% using the built in controls

You could demo 50% 100% and 20%

Drag out the blocks as shown below

Write the algorithm up somewhere as shown

Algorith plan
Start green flag
Wait until touching fish
Say things
End the game

Can they create and order the blocks to make this happen?

As they do this, go round and check the order

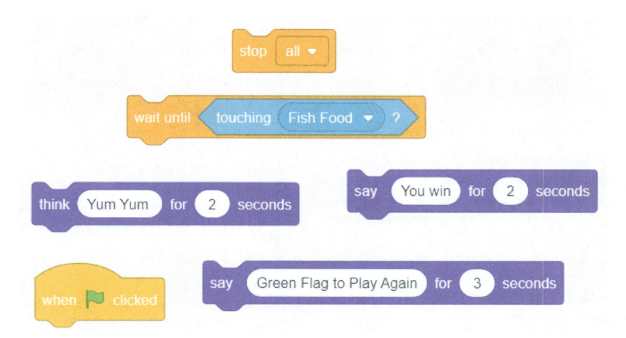

15. Final instructions

Paint a new sprite

Use text tool to type the instructions

Use paint brush tool to paint blob of contrasting colour behind text.

Use layering tool to move blob behind

Encourage pupils to create their own instructions

Front   Back

Layering Tool

16. Code instructions

In the instruction sprite

Drag out the code blocks as shown on the right

Explain that we want the instructions to

Show when i key pressed

Wait for 10 seconds then hide

Can they work out the right order?

Display somewhere pupils can see it

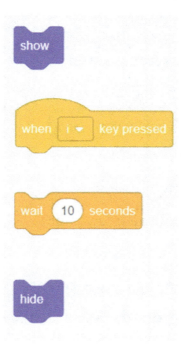

After giving them time to attempt this, show pupils the correct finished code solution.

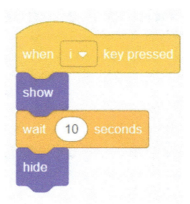

Finished Code

Decompose Fish Fun Game

List the objects you will need to make this game

Tick all the things the game does at the moment

☐ Move when the 1 key is pressed

☐ Move further when the 2 key is pressed

☐ Darken the background when the k key is pressed

☐ Turn to the right when right arrow key is pressed

☐ Spin round when the s key is pressed

☐ Turn to the left when the left arrow key is pressed

☐ Grow the fish when the b key is pressed

☐ Leave a trail when fish moves

☐ Say thing when touching Fish Food

☐ Stop leaving a trail when the u key is pressed

☐ Clear all lines when the e key is pressed

☐ Show instructions when the i key is pressed

☐ Change to a new background when green flag is clicked

☐ Shrink the fish when the t key is pressed

☐ Fish swims side to side when 1 or 2 key pressed

What would you add to the game?

Decomposing Fish Fun Game Marksheet

List the objects you will need to make this game
Carp sprite, instructions, backgrounds, Fish food, start (1 mark for any two of these)

Tick all the things the game does at the moment

☑ Move when the 1 key is pressed (1 mark)

☑ Move further when the 2 key is pressed (1 mark)

☐ Darken the background when the k key is pressed (-1 mark)

☑ Turn to the right when right arrow key is pressed (1 mark)

☐ Spin round when the s key is pressed (-1 mark)

☑ Turn to the left when the left arrow key is pressed (1 mark)

☐ Grow the fish when the b key is pressed (-1 mark)

☑ Leave a trail when fish moves (1 mark)

☑ Say thing when touching Fish Food (1 mark)

☑ Stop leaving a trail when the u key is pressed (1 mark)

☑ Clear all lines when the e key is pressed (1 mark)

☑ Show instructions when the i key is pressed (1 mark)

☑ Change to a new background when green flag is clicked (1 mark)

☐ Shrink the fish when the t key is pressed (-1 mark)

☑ Fish swims side to side when 1 or 2 key pressed (1 mark)

What would you add to the game?
Any reasonable answer (1 mark)

photocopiable page

55

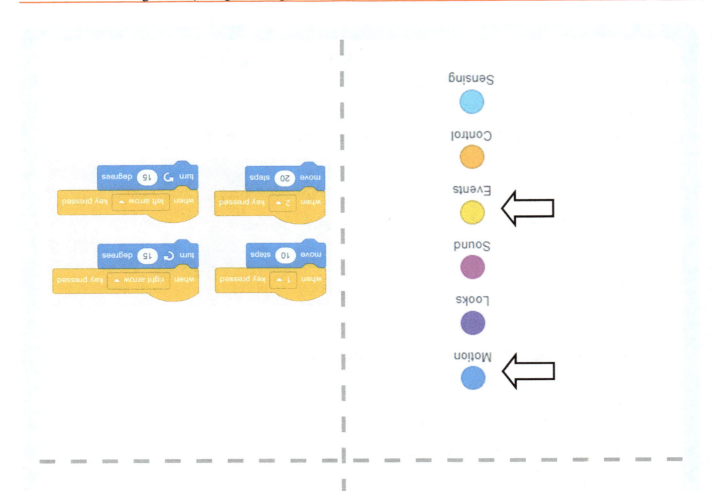

Moving and Steering Back

Moving and Steering

photocopiable page

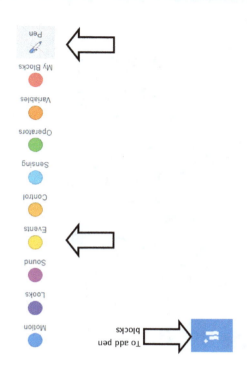

Pen up, pen down, erase all back

Pen up
Pen down
Erase all

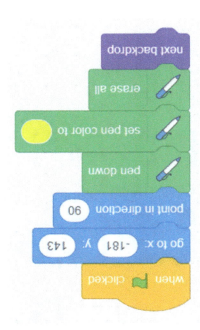

Initialization back

Initialization

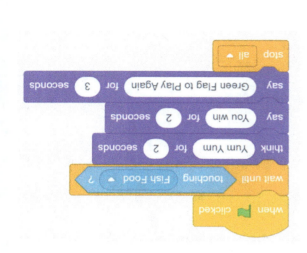

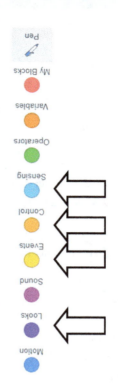

End Game Back

End Game

photocopiable page

> **Overview**
> Pupils learn about simple sequence away from computers if they have not already done so. Pupils examine different animations techniques in full screen mode and predict how they are created as a class. Teacher demos one, and pupils make their own version. Repeat for all versions.

To do before the session

1. Look at the grid below to see the order of learning
2. Print pupil worksheets for each activity if there is one, worksheet column
3. Print marksheets for activities if it has one to be placed where pupils can access them. If it has a worksheet, it has a pupil marksheet.
4. Download the code needed and place in a templates folder on your school network or add to a Scratch Studio or link on your learning platform.
5. Download the slides that go with the concept introduction
6. Study the notes that go with the slides
7. Examine the teacher help notes that are provided with every activity

To do at the start of the session

If you have not introduced simple sequence with this class before do this first using the slides as a whole class activity.

To do after the concept has been introduced

Each activity has whole class notes to help you explain what is needed if it is the first time pupils have carried out this type of activity. There are also core instruction underneath in case you are sticking to the core activities only.

How this module fits into a programming progression

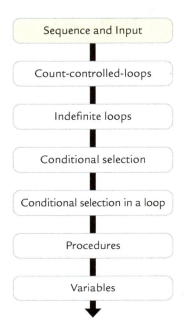

Sequence and Input

Count-controlled-loops

Indefinite loops

Conditional selection

Conditional selection in a loop

Procedures

Variables

Resource Name	Core Optional SEN	Teacher	Pupil Grouping	How Assessed	HAS Work-sheet	SCRATCH ACCESS
CONCEPT Simple Sequence & fast and slow blocks	**CORE**	Leads Session	Solo whole class activity	Formative	NO	NO
PREDICT	**CORE**	Support Poor Readers	Paired	Pupil marked marksheet provided	YES	NO
CHANGE	**CORE**	Whole class activity	Solo or paired	Formative assessment	NO	YES
I DO YOU DO	**CORE**	Teacher demos animation method pupils adapt it	Solo	Pupils self assessment checked by teacher	NO	YES

Vocabulary
Sequence, order, arrange, pause, block, script

Key Programming Knowledge

Key Sequence Knowledge

The order actions/instructions are arranged in is a sequence

Algorithmic Knowledge

- I can make my instructions more precise so that they are more likely to be followed exactly as I wanted them to be
- I can finish my instructions so no one will be in doubt as to what they do
- When planning an algorithm that will be converted into code I will consider what type of instructions can be turned into code and use these

Algorithmic Knowledge

- I am careful to order my sequence as I know that the same blocks ordered in a different way will produce different outcomes
- I can include wait commands in sequences to slow down the speed that blocks without timings are run in Scratch
- I can choose a way to start my sequence that might involve a keyboard, mouse or trackpad input so they can be run

Resources

Online Resources
Animation Examples
https://scratch.mit.edu/projects/636793709/

English Computing National Curriculum Programs of Study

Pupils should be taught to:

➢ **design, write and debug programs that accomplish specific goals,** including controlling or simulating physical systems; solve problems by decomposing them into smaller parts

➢ **use sequence,** selection and repetition in programs; work with variables **and various forms of input and output**

➢ **use logical reasoning to explain how some simple algorithms work and to detect and correct errors in algorithms and programs**

Scottish Curriculum for Excellence Technologies

- I understand the instructions of a visual programming language and can predict the outcome of a program written using the language. TCH 1-14a
- I can explain core programming language concepts in appropriate technical language TCH 2-14a
- I can demonstrate a range of basic problem solving skills by building simple programs to carry out a given task, using an appropriate language. TCH 1-15a
- I can create, develop and evaluate computing solutions in response to a design challenge. TCH 2-15a

Welsh National Curriculum Relevant Strands

Progression Step 3.

- I can use conditional statements to add control and decision-making to algorithms.
- I can explain and debug algorithms.

1. Prediction

Give out the animation prediction sheets found on p64 one between two pupils.

Instruct pupils to read the code with their partner carefully and then choose a prediction 1 2 or 3.

If they disagree with their partner they can tick different boxes and mark their initiuals by their prediction. There are teacher help notes on page 65.

Once pupils have done this use the marking sheet on page 69 to mark this.

Animation Prediction

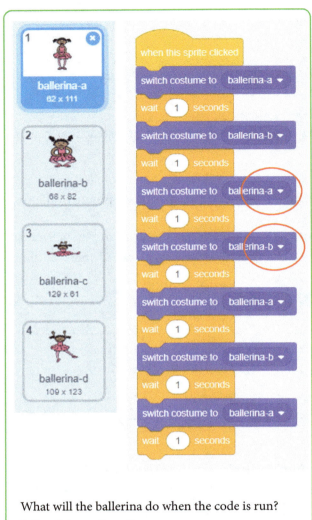

What will the ballerina do when the code is run?

1. Bend down three times
2. Do the splits three times
3. Raise hands three times

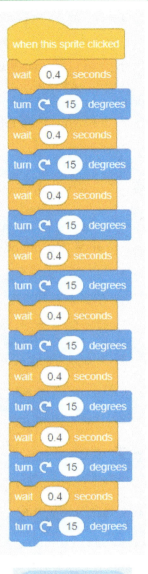

What will the soccer ball do when the code is run?

1. Bounce up and down
2. Burst
3. Roll

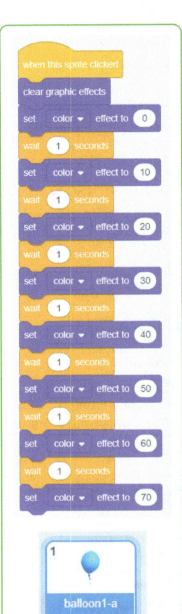

What will the balloon do when the code is run?

1. Pop
2. Change colour
3. Fly away

photocopiable page

Animation Prediction Teacher Support

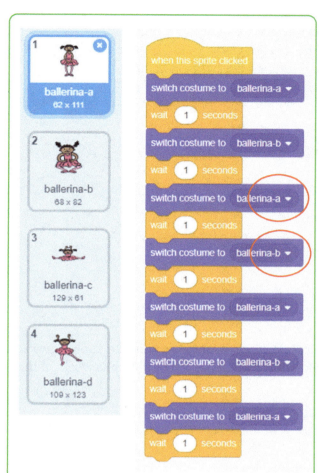

What will the ballerina do when the code is run?

1. Bend down three times (1 mark)
2. Do the splits three times
3. Raise hands three times

Ballerina Help

Make a big point of reading the switch costumes and then finding the correct costume on the left. This helps them to see that it is changing from A to B and not running any other costume.

Prediction Notes

A lot of pupils miss clues because they don't read the code.

You might want to model reading the code with the ballerina sprite example with the whole class. See Ballerina Help to do this.

What will the soccer ball do when the code is run?

1. Bounce up and down
2. Burst
3. Turn round (1 mark)

Soccer Ball Help

If pupils are unsure ask them what they think the curved arrow will do after the turn word.

What will the balloon do when the code is run?

1. Pop
2. Change colour (1 mark)
3. Fly away

Balloon Help

If pupils are unsure ask them what clues there are in the code? Is popping, flying or colour mentioned in the code?

Whole Class Change Questions

Now ask pupils to start Scratch and load the animation demo

http://scratch.mit.edu/project/636793709

You can work in pairs or solo depending on how much support you want pupils to have.

Explain to the class that you are now going to give them some challenges to change. Once they have solved one, they can come and tell you what they did and you can give them the next challenge.

1. Can they make the bear walk slower?

Answer change 0.2 seconds to a higher number

2. Can they make the ballerina high kick instead of bending down?

Answer change all ballerina-b to ballerina-c

3. Can they make the soccer ball bounce faster?

Answer change 0.4 to 0.3, 0.2 or 0.1 (hundredths would work too)

4. Can they make the nodding girl nod faster without changing the wait blocks?

Answer just use nod1 and nod3

Teacher Animation Demo

Ask pupils to create an empty copy of scratch (File/New). Explain that you are now going to show how each type of animation was created and then they can go and make their own better version. Pupils work on their own in the section.

Work order

Teacher demo change picture in sequence

Pupils make a costume change adaptation

Teacher demo make a ball bounce

Pupils make bouncing adaptation

Teacher demo make a ball roll

Pupils make something else roll

Teacher demo move a part

Pupils make move a part adaptation

Teacher demo build a picture

Pupils make build a picture adaptation

You could also print out the animation techniques and ask some pupils to use these to create an animation themselves although this method is harder and you might want to reserve it for your most able programmers.

Change Pictures in Sequence

This is the easiest one to do but sprites must have multiple costumes to make it work.

Hover over the sprite when choosing it. If it changes, it has more than one costume.

The bear and the ballet dancer are great examples of sprites with multiple costumes are already created.

The programmer only needs to change these with suitable pauses to create great animations.

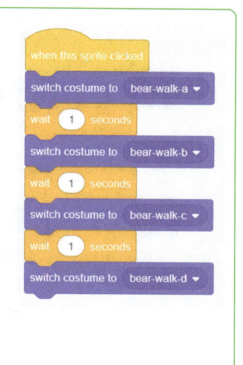

Making a ball bounce

Import a ball sprite

Right click to duplicate the sprite.

On the second sprite, drag a box around the whole costume.

Move it up or down from the middle.

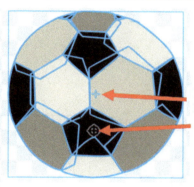

New Centre higher up

Original Centre

Making a ball roll

Use the turn right or turn left blocks.

Changing Colour

Use the set colour effects blocks.

Make sure you change the number.

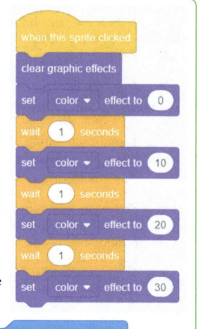

Move a Part

Select Part

In Scratch 3, you can break up parts of the pictures by left clicking and dragging a box around the parts that you want to use.

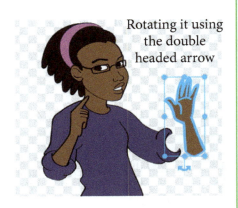

Selecting a hand by dragging a box around it

Rotate

These also have a double-headed arrow at the bottom so you can rotate the part you have selected.

Rotating it using the double headed arrow

Move & Resize

You can move the part by holding it in the middle and resize it from the corner and side manipulation points.

Build a Picture

The house is made by starting with an empty sprite and renaming the first costume as house.

Drawing the first part of the picture in this case the base line.

Then duplicating the sprite (right mouse and duplicate) and adding more details before duplicating and repeating the previous steps.

Novice programmers often exclude the initialization of the sprite costumes and the need to start at the first picture.

Renaming first costume

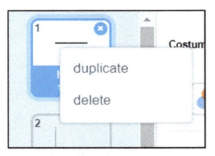

Duplicate Costumes

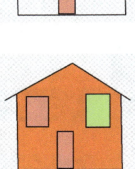

photocopiable page

Animation Predication Teacher support – Page 63

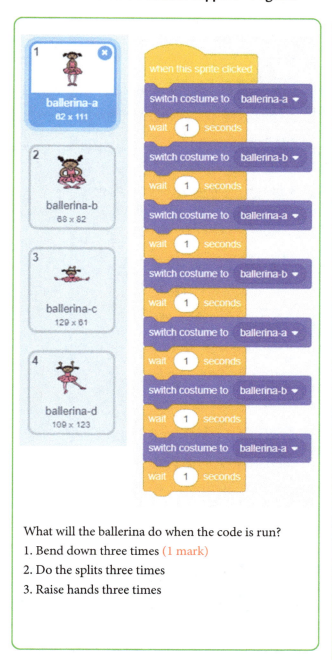

What will the ballerina do when the code is run?

1. Bend down three times (1 mark)
2. Do the splits three times
3. Raise hands three times

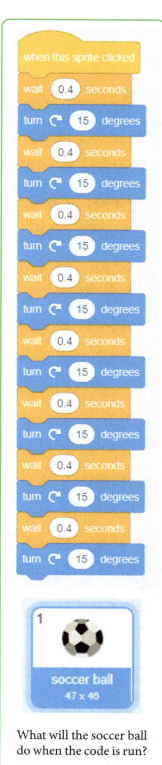

What will the soccer ball do when the code is run?

1. Bounce up and down
2. Burst
3. Roll (1 mark)

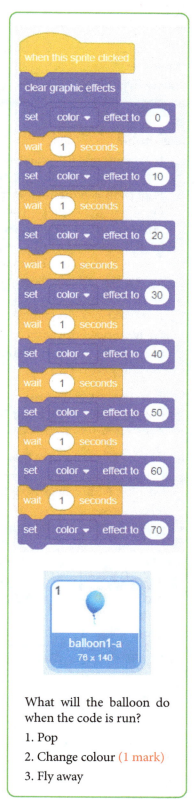

What will the balloon do when the code is run?

1. Pop
2. Change colour (1 mark)
3. Fly away

photocopiable page

Overview

Explore a pre-made game using the PRIMM methodology. Pupils will have their own booklets to record their answers, and teachers will have marksheets for every stage that pupils can use independently.

To do before the session

1. Look at the grid below and decide which optional activities you are going to include and exclude
2. Print pupil worksheets for each activity chosen and staple into a booklet one for each pupil
3. Print marksheets for activities chosen to be placed where pupils can access them
4. Download the code needed and place in a templates folder on your school network or add to a Scratch Studio or link on your learning platform
5. Download the slides that go with the concept introduction
6. Study the notes that go with the slides
7. Examine the teacher help notes that are provided alongside every activity

To do at the start of the session

If you have not introduced simple sequence with this class before, do this first as a whole class activity

To do after the concept has been introduced

Each activity has whole class notes to help you explain what is needed if it is the first time pupils have carried out this type of activity. There is also core instruction underneath in case you are sticking to the core activities only.

How this module fits into a programming progression

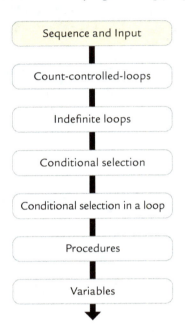

| Sequence and Input |
| Count-controlled-loops |
| Indefinite loops |
| Conditional selection |
| Conditional selection in a loop |
| Procedures |
| Variables |

Resource Name	Core Optional	Teacher	Pupil Grouping	How Assessed	SCRATCH ACCESS
CONCEPT Simple Sequence	CORE	Leads session	Solo whole class activity	Formative	NO
PREDICT	OPTIONAL	Support poor readers	Paired	Pupil marked marksheet provided	NO
INVESTIGATE	CORE	Support poor readers	Paired	Pupil marked marksheet provided	YES
CHANGE	CORE	Support poor readers	paired	Pupil marked marksheet provided	YES
CREATE	CORE	Assesses pupil work and checks pupil self-assessment	Solo	Pupil assessed & teacher assessed	YES

Vocabulary

Sequence: Order, actions, run, code, script, algorithm

Core activities general instructions

1. Group pupils in roughly same ability pairs. For **investigate** and **change** worksheets, pupils will work in pairs, for **create** they will work separately.

2. Give out the pupil booklets and explain that pupils need to follow the instructions on the sheets to explore how **sequence** works.

3. Explain that each pupil will record separately while working alongside their partner and keeping to the same pace as their partner.

4. Demonstrate where they can find the template code and explain that pupils will share one device for investigate and change.

5. Explain that during each question only one person should touch the shared device, and they should swap who that person is when there is a new questions.

6. Encourage them to discuss their answers with their partner. If they disagree with their partner, they can record a different answer in their own booklet.

7. Show pupils where it says they should mark their work on the sheet where the answer sheets are in the classroom.

8. Remind pupils to return marksheets after marking because there are not enough for every pair to have their own.

Key Sequence Knowledge
The order actions/instructions are arranged in is a sequence

Algorithmic Knowledge
I can make my instructions more precise so that they are more likely to be followed exactly as I wanted them to be
I can finish my instructions so no one will be in doubt as to what they do
When planning an algorithm that will be converted into code I will consider what type of instructions can be turned into code and use these

Programming Knowledge
I am careful to order my sequence as I know that the same blocks ordered in a different way will produce different outcomes
I can include wait commands in sequences to slow down the speed that blocks without timings are run in Scratch
I can choose a way to start my sequence that might involve a keyboard, mouse or trackpad input so they can be run

Resources
Ladybug Munch   https://scratch.mit.edu/projects/327508855/

 On the sheet if it says no Scratch, they must work only on the sheet,

 If it says Scratch with a green tick, they can use one device between the pair.

 If it says work with a partner, they must work at the same speed as their partner.

 If it says work on their own, they must do this using a separate device each working alone.

English Computing National Curriculum Programs of Study
Pupils should be taught to:

- **design, write and debug programs that accomplish specific goals,** including controlling or simulating physical systems; solve problems by decomposing them into smaller parts

- **use sequence,** selection and repetition in programs; work with variables **and various forms of input and output**

- **use logical reasoning to explain how some simple algorithms work and to detect and correct errors in algorithms and programs**

Scottish Curriculum for Excellence Technologies
I understand the instructions of a visual programming language and can predict the outcome of a program written using the language. TCH 1-14a

I can explain core programming language concepts in appropriate technical language TCH 2-14a

I can demonstrate a range of basic problem solving skills by building simple programs to carry out a given task, using an appropriate language. TCH 1-15a

I can create, develop and evaluate computing solutions in response to a design challenge. TCH 2-15a

Welsh National Curriculum Relevant Strands
Progression Step 3

- I can use conditional statements to add control and decision-making to algorithms.

- I can explain and debug algorithms.

Ladybug Munch Game

PREDICT

Work with a partner

Draw a line to match the code to what it does. One has been done for you

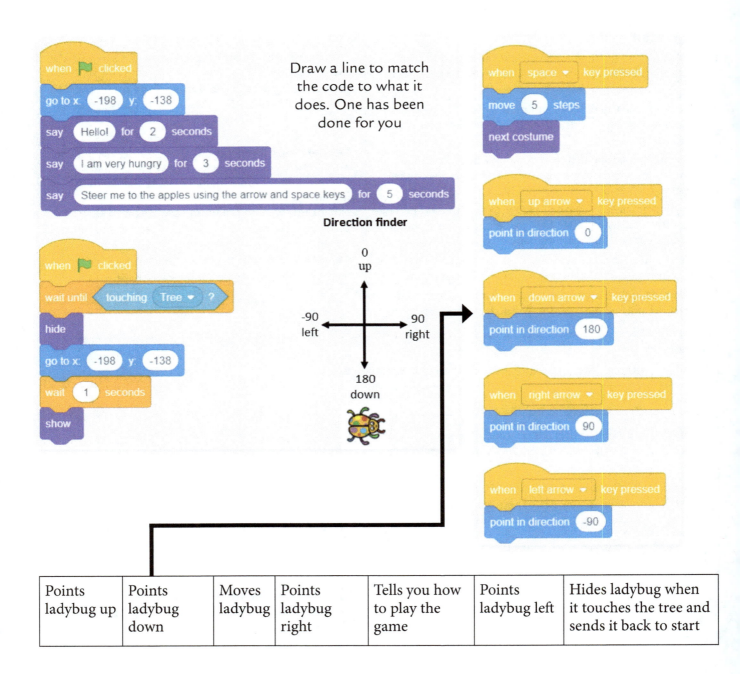

Direction finder

0
up

-90
left

90
right

180
down

Points ladybug up	Points ladybug down	Moves ladybug	Points ladybug right	Tells you how to play the game	Points ladybug left	Hides ladybug when it touches the tree and sends it back to start

Now start Scratch, load the
Ladybug program and run the code to see if you were right.

Mark your predictions above.

PREDICT TEACHER SUPPORT

WHOLE CLASS ADVICE

Make sure you work with your partner on this sheet. Take it in turns to read a section and tell your partner what you think it does. Then answer the questions using your understanding of the code.

NOTES ON THE ACTIVITY

This optional activity helps pupils to think about what the code does before running it.

ALL

Ask pupils to look for key words or symbols that might help them establish what the code does? Can they find those key words or symbols in the code or descriptions?

SEND ADVICE

Use a book to cover up parts of the code so pupils can only focus on a few choices at a time.

If working on point the ladybug up cover up the longer bits of code on the left.

ALL

Remind pupils that the direction finder is in the middle to help them understand the point in direction blocks. It acts as a key.

ALL

If pupils are confused by the x and y blocks, explain that they refer to places on the screen and they will learn more about these in later years.

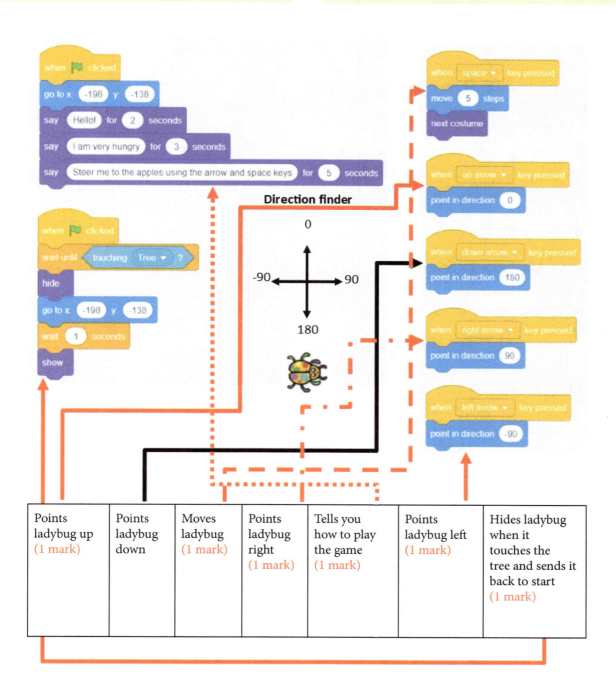

Points ladybug up (1 mark)	Points ladybug down	Moves ladybug (1 mark)	Points ladybug right (1 mark)	Tells you how to play the game (1 mark)	Points ladybug left (1 mark)	Hides ladybug when it touches the tree and sends it back to start (1 mark)

Ladybug Munch Game
INVESTIGATE

Work with a partner

Play the game a few times. Start it with the green flag.

Run and Investigate (Run the programs to help you answer the questions)

Look at the code inside the Ladybug

Ladybug Sprite Questions

1. What **key** will point the ladybug 180 degrees?

2. What **key** will move the Ladybug five steps and change her costume?

3. What **direction** will the Ladybug point in when the **up arrow key** is pressed? (up, down, right or left)

Look at the code inside the Apple

Apple Sprite Questions

4. What **size** (%) is the apple set to?

5. Which costume is run **first**?

6. What **code** makes the costume change to **applehalf**?

7. For how many **seconds** does the program show the **applehalf** costume before hiding?

Now mark your work using the answer sheet

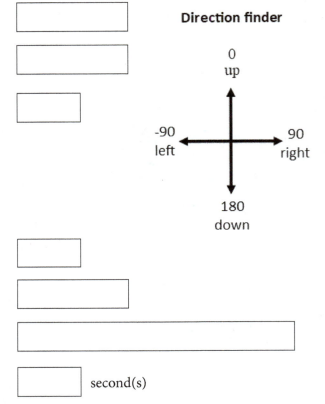

Direction finder

```
              0
             up

-90                    90
left                   right

             180
            down
```

second(s)

Total	/7

INVESTIGATE TEACHER HELPSHEET

WHOLE CLASS ADVICE

Work in pairs, one device between the pair. Take it in turns every question to swap who runs code. You must work at the same pace as your partner and not move on to the next question until you have both written your answer down. If you disagree, write a different answer. You must mark your work before moving on to the next section with your partner.

NOTES ON THE ACTIVITY

Investigating the code encourages pupils to think deeply about how it works. Check that every pupil is filling in and marking the questions individually but at the pace of the slowest in the pair. Sometimes a pair decides not to mark to speed up their efforts. Marking gives valuable information so I recommend sending them back to mark their work. A class instruction to come and talk to you if they have over half of the questions wrong or they do not understand the answer after they have marked it helps to check progress is being made correctly. There is real value in collecting these scores to build up a summative picture of pupil progress.

SEND ADVICE

Support pairs of pupils who are poor readers by reading questions, reading code samples and covering up questions until they get to them.

SEN HELP

SEN often miss out on the page clues as to which sprite to be looking at when answering a question.

Questions 1

Can pupils find 180 in the code what key makes the 180 block work?

Questions 2

Can pupils find five steps in the code? Explain that 1 step is one pixel or dot on the screen

Play the game a few times. Start it with the green flag.

USE (Run the programs lots of times but don't change the code)

Look at the code inside the Ladybug

Ladybug Sprite Questions

1. What **key** will point the ladybug 180 degrees?

   down arrow

2. What **key** will move the Ladybug five steps and change her costume?

   space

3. What **direction** will the Ladybug point in when the **up arrow key** is pressed? (up, down, right or left)

   up

Look at the code inside the Apple

Apple Sprite Questions

4. What **size** (%) is the apple set to?

   50%

5. Which costume is run **first**?

   applewhole

6. What **code** makes the costume change to **applehalf**?

   Switch costume to applehalf

7. For how many **seconds** does the program show the **applehalf** costume before hiding?

   1   second(s)

Questions 3

Hint, they can either press the key and see what happens or click on the point in direction 0 number and see what pops up.

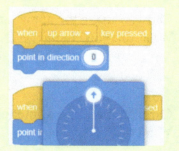

Questions 4

Clue look for % sign.

Questions 5

Remind pupil that code always starts at the top and works its way to the bottom.

Questions 6

Clues here are in the sequence

Show applehalf

Hide

Use your finger to point out that portion of the code

**Ladybug Munch Game
CHANGE**

Work with a partner

CHANGE (Run the code and make small changes)

Ladybug Sprite Questions

1. Can you make the Ladybug **say its name** at the beginning of the game?
   What did you change? *HINT Say block*

2. Can you make the Ladybug **move further** every time the space key is pressed?
   What did you change?

3. Can you **stop** the Ladybug looking like it is wiggling its legs when it moves?
   What did you change? *HINT Remove a block HINT Costumes*

4. Can you make the Ladybug hide for longer once it touches the tree?
   What did you change?

Apple Sprite Questions

5. Can you make the apple **larger**?
   What did you change? *HINT %*

6. Can you make the **applehalf** costume stay on stage for a **longer time**?
   What did you change?

Now mark this page using the answer sheet

CHANGE TEACHER SUPPORT

WHOLE CLASS ADVICE

Work in pairs, one device between the pair. Take it in turns every question to swap who runs code. You must work at the same pace as your partner and not move on to the next question until you have both written your answer down. If you disagree, write a different answer. You must mark your work before moving on to the next section.

NOTES ON THE ACTIVITY

Changing or modifying code is a core part of this module so I suggest you do not leave it out. It is an important step towards creation of their own code as parts they have modified they will feel more ownership of. Recording marks will help with assessment.

Question 1 Pupils need to adapt or add to this section of code. They could change Hello to Hello I am Ladybug or similar or add a new say block.

HINTS Might include where is the code does it introduce the game.

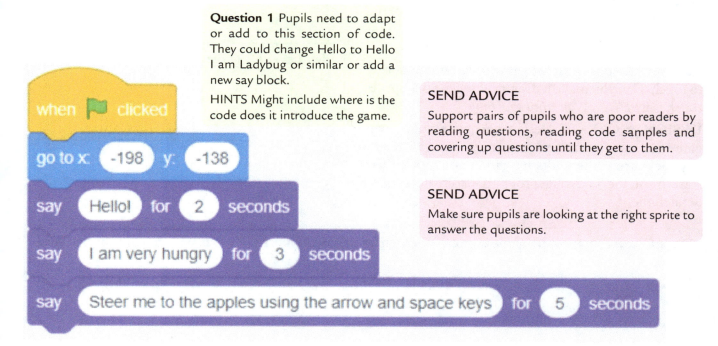

SEND ADVICE

Support pairs of pupils who are poor readers by reading questions, reading code samples and covering up questions until they get to them.

SEND ADVICE

Make sure pupils are looking at the right sprite to answer the questions.

Ladybug Sprite Questions

1. Can you make the Ladybug say its name at the beginning of the game? What did you change?

   Either add text to say blocks or add a new say or think block (1 mark)

2. Can you make the Ladybug move further every time the space key is pressed? What did you change?

   Change move five steps to a higher number or add another move so many steps underneath the first one (1 mark)

3. Can you stop the Ladybug looking like it is wiggling its legs when it moves ? What did you change?

   Remove the next costume block (1 mark)

4. Can you make the Ladybug hide for longer once it touches the tree? What did you change?

   Change wait 1 second to a higher number (1 mark)

Apple Sprite Questions

5. Can you make the apple larger? What did you change?

   Change set size to a higher number than 50% (1 mark)

6. Can you make the applehalf costume stay on stage for longer? What did you change?

   Change wait 1 second to a higher number (1 mark)

Questions 3

Show pupils the two costumes in the costume tab. Click on both to show them how they are different and changing from one to the other looks like the legs are moving / walking. These are small changes so not every pupil will have noticed the effect.

Questions 4

Hint

Where is the code block that makes it hide?

How long does it hide for at the moment? A 1 second

Questions 5

A few minutes introducing % can be useful: 100% is full size, 50% is half size, 200% is twice as big.

Questions 6

Point out that longer is a time word. Can they find any time words in the code, hours, minutes, seconds, etc.?

Ladybug Munch Game
Make

Work with a partner

You can share design ideas but must plan and code separately

Make First

Add another sprite into the ladybug munch game. Can you make it move and steer using letter keys? *HINT When key pressed HINT Use different keys to the ladybug*

Make Second

Add another sprite into the game for your new sprite to touch. Can you make it disappear when your sprite touches it? *HINT Wait until touching*

DESIGN & CREATE Design and code your own game that uses inputs and sequences. You can adapt any ideas from the Ladybug game. You can either start from the Ladybug program or create a new Scratch file.

> **Idea Level** *My game will…*

> **Design Level** Draw your game simply, What characters will you use? What will they do? What commands will you use?

Teacher & Pupil Assessment

Circle one column on each row to show what you think you have achieved

	Not used any code	Copied code from the ladybug munch game	Copied and changed code from ladybug munch game	Created own code not shown in ladybug munch game (can include ideas from other projects)
Code	0 Marks	1 mark	2 marks	3 marks

(Only to be used if make second has been planned and created)	No theme in planning or code	Has a theme in planning or code
Has a project theme in planning or code	0 Marks	1 mark

SUPPORTING CREATE

WHOLE CLASS ADVICE

Work on your own, one device each. You can discuss the work with your former partner but you are responsible for creating your own projects. Save your work regularly. Read the instructions carefully. Assess your own work by circling where you think you are in the assessment grid at the bottom of the page.

NOTES ON THE ACTIVITY

The make part of a project is really important, and teachers should always make sure that pupils have time to make their own project even if that means reducing the time spent on other stages for pupils who work slowly. It helps if pupils work on their own for this whilst supporting their partner.

Create First

Add another sprite into the ladybug munch game. Can you make it move and steer using letter keys? *HINT When key pressed HINT Use different keys to the ladybug*

Create Second

Add another sprite into the game for your new sprite to touch. Can you make it disappear when your sprite touches it? *HINT Wait until touching*

DESIGN & CREATE Design and code your own game that uses inputs and sequences. You can adapt any ideas from the Ladybug game. You can either start from the Ladybug program or create a new Scratch file.

Idea Level *My game will…*

Design Level Draw your game simply, What characters will you use? What will they do? What commands will you use?

Design Level Teacher Guidance

Getting pupils to show you their designs first before building can be a great way of promoting the importance of design and stopping pupils missing this important thinking step.

Create First Pupil Support

Looking at the code examples in Ladybug Munch always help

Create Second SEN

If a pupil is struggling you might drag out these blocks but don't connect them to help them think about the order

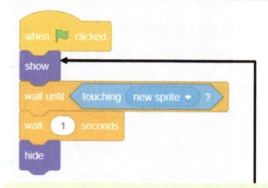

Create Second Pupil Support

Pupils often forget to include the show as they forget it will need to show before it can work every time. Show is an example of initialization.

SEN

SEN pupils could tell you about the game instead of writing about it.

Assessment Guidance

Assessing before the end of a project enables you to give feedback and points pupils can improve before a final assessment at the end of the project.

Teacher & Pupil Assessment

Circle one column on each row to show what you think you have achieved

	Not used any code	Copied code from the ladybug munch game	Copied and changed code from ladybug munch game	Created own code not shown in ladybug munch game (can include ideas from other projects)
Code	0 Marks	1 mark	2 marks	3 marks

(Only to be used if make second has been planned and created)	No theme in planning or code	Has a theme in planning or code
Has a project theme in planning or code	0 Marks	1 mark

Ladybug Munch – Page 71

Predict

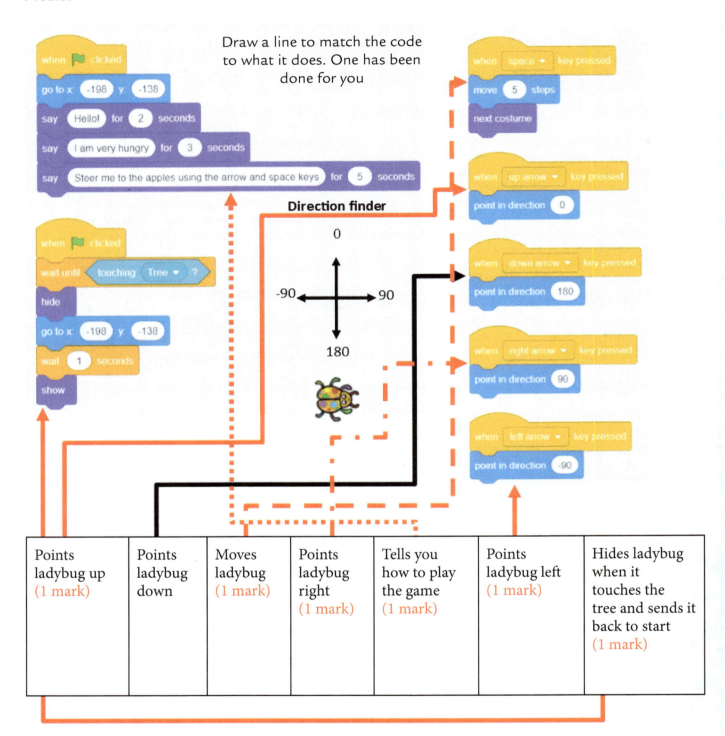

Draw a line to match the code to what it does. One has been done for you

Direction finder

Points ladybug up (1 mark)	Points ladybug down	Moves ladybug (1 mark)	Points ladybug right (1 mark)	Tells you how to play the game (1 mark)	Points ladybug left (1 mark)	Hides ladybug when it touches the tree and sends it back to start (1 mark)

Investigate

Play the game a few times. Start it with the green flag.

USE (Run the programs lots of times but don't change the code)

Look at the code inside the Ladybug
Ladybug Sprite Questions

1. What **key** will point the ladybug 180 degrees?

    down arrow

2. What **key** will move the Ladybug five steps and change her costume?

    space

3. What **direction** will the Ladybug point in when the **up arrow key** is pressed? (up, down, right or left)

    up

Look at the code inside the Apple
Apple Sprite Questions

4. What **size** (%) is the apple set to?

    50%

5. Which costume is run **first**?

    applewhole

6. What **code** makes the costume change to **applehalf**?

    Switch costume to applehalf

7. For how many **seconds** does the program show the **applehalf** costume before hiding?

    1   second(s)

1 mark for every correct answer

Ladybug Sprite Questions

1. Can you make the Ladybug say its name at the beginning of the game? What did you change?

   Either add text to say blocks or add a new say or think block (1 mark)

2. Can you make the Ladybug move further every time the space key is pressed? What did you change?

   Change move five steps to a higher number or add another move so many steps underneath the first one (1 mark)

3. Can you stop the Ladybug looking like it is wiggling its legs when it moves ? What did you change?

   Remove the next costume block (1 mark)

4. Can you make the Ladybug hide for longer once it touches the tree? What did you change?

   Change wait 1 second to a higher number (1 mark)

Apple Sprite Questions

5. Can you make the apple larger? What did you change?

   Change set size to a higher number than 50% (1 mark)

6. Can you make the applehalf costume stay on stage for longer? What did you change?

   Change wait 1 second to a higher number (1 mark)